My Favorite Monster

Story by Erica Galloway
Illustrations by Jacqui C. Smith

What's your favorite color?
Blue.

What's your favorite flower?
A Sunflower.

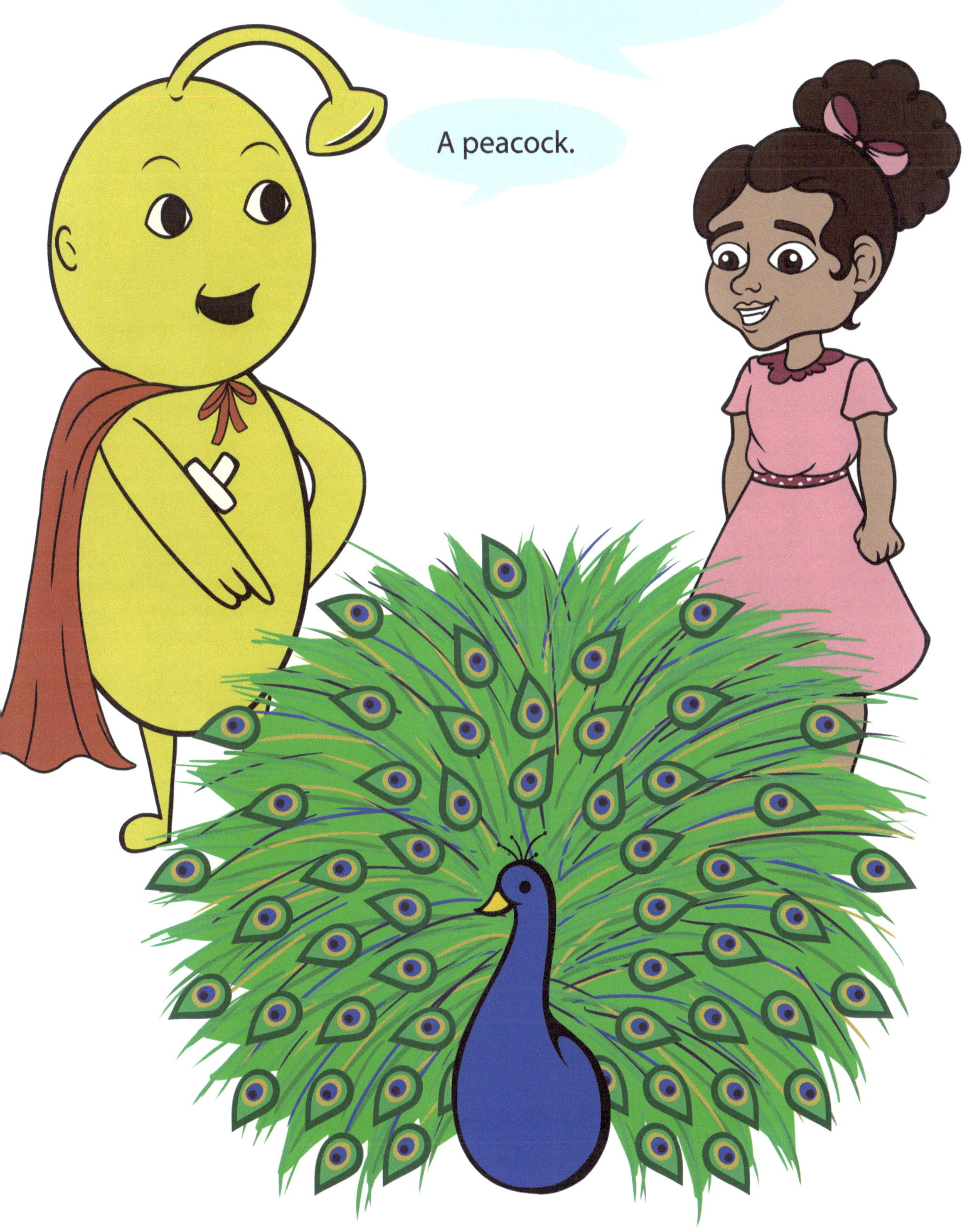
What's your favorite animal?
A peacock.

What's your favorite fish?
An octopus.

What is your favorite book?
This book, because we are in it.
Good answer.
My Favorite Monster

Who is your favorite monster?
Ummm…..
Ummmmmm…..

I'm not your favorite monster?

Well, I don't know any other monsters to say if you are my favorite or not.

But I have a cape. I'm smart, and I'm helping you become a better person.
Yeah, but what if other monsters did that too?

I have an idea. Let's hold
a monster audition.

Fine.
Fine.

FAVORITE MONSTER AUDITION

DO YOU HAVE WHAT IT TAKES
TO BE HEIDI'S FAVORITE MONSTER?

FAVORITE
MONSTERS
AUDITION

I'm a ballerina monster! I can twirl, and, twirl, and twirl
NEXT!
That's it? I've practiced my whole life for this.
We will be in touch.
DIRECTOR
DIRECTOR
No we won't.

I thought I had what it takes.

ROAR!

I'm a scary monster and
I can scare all the bad people away.

But you're so cute.

No I'm Not!

DIRECTOR
Anger Issues.
DIRECTOR

I'm a monster, and my talent is eating cookies
Do you live in a garbage can too?
That wasn't funny.

My name is Monscassco
Like piscassco, but better.
NEXT!

You're welcome.
Don't call me. I'll call you.

They call me spider monster.
I'm a monster but I have
the powers of a spider.

NEXT!

I do monster things no other monster can do.

I eat my vegetables to stay strong.

I can count to 1,000.

I can be mean.

I can be happy.

I choose my attitude.

I'll help you with your homework.
I'll help you clean up your room...
I'm your favorite monster.
I can even say my ABC's backwards.
ZYXWVU

I can't say my ABC's backward.

I guess I'll go pack my things"

No wait.

You're my BEST Friend, and no other Monster
makes me laugh the way you do,
and no one cares for me the way you do.

Of all of the monsters,
you are MY favorite monster!

What a waste.
And you're my favorite human!
The End.